WHEN YOUR CHURCH FEELS

STUCK

STUDY GUIDE

Cover design: Sara Young
Cover photo: Brenton Stanley

ISBN: 978-1-960678-44-7   1 2 3 4 5 6 7 8 9 10

Printed in the United States of America

WHEN YOUR CHURCH FEELS

STUCK

7 UNAVOIDABLE QUESTIONS
EVERY LEADER MUST ANSWER

STUDY GUIDE

CHRIS SONKSEN

ARROWS &
STONES

CONTENTS

WHEN YOUR CHURCH FEELS

STUCK

7 UNAVOIDABLE QUESTIONS
EVERY LEADER MUST ANSWER

STUDY GUIDE

CHRIS SONKSEN

MY CHURCH IS STUCK

*We have to be willing to explore
new ways of doing things and, more
importantly, new ways of thinking.*

READING TIME

As you read Chapter 1: "My Church Is Stuck" in *When Your Church Feels Stuck*, review, reflect on, and respond to the text by answering the following questions.

REFLECT AND TAKE ACTION:

Is your church currently stuck? In what ways? What is holding you back?

_____

_____

_____

_____

_____

_____

Have you helped your church get unstuck in the past? If so, what did it become unstuck from, and how did you do it?

_____

_____

_____

_____

_____

_____

_____

What did you learn from the story told at the beginning of this chapter?

_____

_____

_____

_____

_____

_____

_____

_____

Which of the three categories of church does yours fall under: "They do everything," "They do anything," or "They do nothing"?

_____

_____

_____

_____

_____

_____

_____

_____

_____

Explain how and why you believe your church is in this category. Are you satisfied with being here?

_____

_____

_____

_____

_____

_____

_____

_____

_____

Are you willing to undergo change and make
sacrifices to get your church unstuck?

_____

_____

_____

_____

_____

_____

_____

What is your vision for the church once it is no longer
stuck?

_____

_____

_____

_____

_____

_____

_____

_____

_____

_____

GOD DETERMINES THE TALENT, WE DETERMINE THE CHOICES

If we don't change, nothing will change.

READING TIME

As you read Chapter 2: "God Determines the Talent, We Determine the Choices" in *When Your Church Feels Stuck*, review, reflect on, and respond to the text by answering the following questions.

REFLECT AND TAKE ACTION:

How do you make choices related to church?

_____

_____

_____

_____

_____

_____

_____

In your own words, how would you define success for a pastor? What about success for the church?

_____

_____

_____

_____

_____

_____

_____

_____

What does "God determines the talent, but we determine the choices" really mean?

_____
_____
_____
_____
_____
_____
_____
_____

Have you ever gotten caught up in the cycle of comparison? With whom were you comparing yourself? How did this make you feel?

_____
_____
_____
_____
_____
_____
_____
_____

Take time to list everything you are a steward of. How can you be a better steward of the things God has entrusted you with?

_____
_____
_____
_____
_____

_____

_____

_____

_____

Whom do you let speak into your life? Do you have a coach or mentor? What's stopping you from getting one?

_____

_____

_____

_____

_____

_____

_____

Are you comfortable with the way things are going in your church? Or, are you pushing yourself and those you lead out of your comfort zones? Explain your answer.

_____

_____

_____

_____

_____

_____

_____

_____

MAKING EXCUSES WILL KEEP YOU FROM WINNING

A good location, greater resources, more programs, big events—all are beneficial, but at their core, they are not sustainable church growth methods.

READING TIME

As you read Chapter 3: "Making Excuses Will Keep You from Winning" in *When Your Church Feels Stuck*, review, reflect on, and respond to the text by answering the following questions.

REFLECT AND TAKE ACTION:

Do you ever get defensive when brought a question or concern? How do you react?

_____

_____

_____

_____

_____

_____

_____

How can you react better to these types of situations?

_____

_____

_____

_____

_____

_____

_____

Which of the categories have you blamed your church's lack of growth on? Your location? Insufficient resources? Lack of big events?

_____

_____

_____

_____

_____

_____

_____

_____

What actually makes a church grow?

_____

_____

_____

_____

_____

_____

_____

_____

Do you look at your leadership as a partnership with God, or are you running the show? If it is a partnership, how often are you going to Him for answers?

_____

_____

_____

_____

_____

_____

_____

_____

_____

Why do you think excuses are so detrimental to improving and growing?

_____

_____

_____

_____

_____

_____

_____

What are some things in the church that you no longer will make excuses regarding? What can you do to improve these areas?

_____

_____

_____

_____

_____

_____

_____

THE SIX PHASES OF A CHURCH . . . WHAT PHASE ARE YOU IN?

You cannot take your church where it needs to be if you can't identify where it is right now.

READING TIME

As you read Chapter 4: "The Six Phases of a Church . . . What Phase Are You In?" in *When Your Church Feels Stuck*, review, reflect on, and respond to the text by answering the following questions.

REFLECT AND TAKE ACTION:

Take time to look over the figure containing the six stages and identify which phase your church is in.

_____

_____

_____

_____

_____

_____

_____

Are you content with the current stage you are in?

_____

_____

_____

_____

_____

_____

_____

_____

Are there any stages of the list you have never experienced? Which are they?

_____

_____

_____

_____

_____

_____

_____

_____

Write out the checklist (listed near the end of each stage description) for your stage below. Do these seem reasonable? How can you achieve them practically?

_____

_____

_____

_____

_____

_____

_____

_____

_____

Why do you feel your church is currently at this stage?

_____

_____

_____

_____

_____

_____

_____

_____

_____

Are there any characteristics your church lost as it grew to another stage? What are they?

_____

_____

_____

_____

_____

_____

_____

What needs to change for you to reach the increase stage?

_____

_____

_____

_____

_____

_____

_____

_____

QUESTION 1— MISSION: *WHAT DO WE DO?*

Remember: [The mission statement] is a statement that will drive it all, so it's important to get it right.

READING TIME

As you read Chapter 5: "Question 1—Mission: What Do We Do?" in *When Your Church Feels Stuck*, review, reflect on, and respond to the text by answering the following questions.

REFLECT AND TAKE ACTION:

Take time to conduct a SWOT analysis. What are the strengths of your church? Your weaknesses? Opportunities? Threats? Talk them out with your team and be honest!

_____

_____

_____

_____

_____

_____

_____

What is your church's mission? How is this portrayed through your church's mission statement?

_____

_____

_____

_____

_____

_____

_____

Can everyone on your church staff recite the church's mission statement?

_____

_____

_____

_____

_____

In what ways do you and your team feel you can improve your current mission statement?

_____

_____

_____

_____

_____

_____

_____

_____

_____

Who will be a part of formulating the new mission statement for the church?

_____

_____

_____

_____

_____

_____

_____

_____

Make time to conduct at least three of the four team exercises provided at the end of this chapter. Then, write what you learn and conclude from each exercise:

God's Heart—Pastor's Heart Exercise:

_____

_____

_____

_____

_____

Discover What Works Exercise:

_____

_____

_____

_____

_____

Discuss the Target Audience Exercise:

_____

_____

_____

_____

_____

Wordsmith Exercise:

_____

_____

_____

_____

QUESTION 2— STRATEGY: *HOW DO WE GET IT DONE?*

Your mission will just be a handful of forgotten words if you don't create a strategy that carries it out.

READING TIME

As you read Chapter 6: "Question 2—Strategy: How Do We Get It Done?" in *When Your Church Feels Stuck*, review, reflect on, and respond to the text by answering the following questions.

REFLECT AND TAKE ACTION:

Does your church have a strategy for achieving its mission? What is it?

_____

_____

_____

_____

_____

_____

_____

How did your church come up with the above strategy? When was the last time it was changed or altered?

_____

_____

_____

_____

_____

_____

_____

_____

What is the difference between programs and processes? What do they each support?

_____

_____

_____

_____

_____

_____

_____

_____

_____

How can you improve your strategy after reading about the "Shallow-Middle-Deep" strategy? Do you split up who you are trying to reach on different levels in any way?

_____

_____

_____

_____

_____

_____

_____

_____

_____

_____

Does your strategy currently answer the question, "How do we do it?" If not, how can you answer this question through your strategy?

_____

_____

_____

_____

_____

_____

_____

_____

_____

Are you intentional about raising up other leaders? Why do you think this is an important aspect of a sustainable church?

_____

_____

_____

_____

_____

_____

_____

_____

_____

CHAPTER 7

QUESTION 3— VALUES:

WHAT ARE THE GUIDING PRINCIPLES WE LIVE BY?

Teach these principles often to your staff and leaders. . . . Look to them often so that they don't become a distant memory. Let them become the guiding principles that help to lead your church to continual and sustainable growth.

READING TIME

As you read Chapter 7: "Question 3—Values: What Are the Guiding Principles We Live By?" in *When Your Church Feels Stuck*, review, reflect on, and respond to the text by answering the following questions.

REFLECT AND TAKE ACTION:

What are your church's values? List them and briefly describe why each item made your list.

_____

_____

_____

_____

_____

_____

_____

Are these values the same for your entire church staff?

_____

_____

_____

_____

_____

_____

_____

Can everyone who works for the church recite these same values?

_____

_____

_____

_____

What is the purpose of having values? What does it do for the church?

_____

_____

_____

_____

_____

_____

Take time to do the "Discovery Phase" exercise provided in this chapter. What topics did you rate the highest? List them here, and take note of whether or not they show up on your original list of values.

_____

_____

_____

_____

_____

_____

_____

_____

_____

Are there any values you think should be added to your list? What are they, and why should they be added?

_____

_____

_____

_____

_____

_____

_____

How have your church's values changed over the years, if at all?

_____

_____

_____

_____

How often do you teach about or voice these values to your church? When can you do this next?

_____

_____

_____

_____

_____

_____

CHAPTER 8

QUESTION 4— METRICS: *HOW DO WE MEASURE A WIN?*

Metrics support the mission.

READING TIME

As you read Chapter 8: "Question 4—Metrics: How Do We Measure a Win?" in *When Your Church Feels Stuck*, review, reflect on, and respond to the text by answering the following questions.

REFLECT AND TAKE ACTION:

What metrics do you use to measure your church's performance? Make a list and briefly describe why you use each metric.

_____

_____

_____

_____

_____

_____

_____

Would you say your church is winning right now or losing? What are the main metrics that measure this?

_____

_____

_____

_____

_____

_____

_____

How are metrics and mission tied together?

_____

_____

_____

_____

_____

_____

_____

_____

_____

_____

What new metrics can you use to determine whether
or not your church is accomplishing its mission?

_____

_____

_____

_____

_____

_____

_____

_____

_____

_____

_____

_____

What would be on your church's dashboard if it were a vehicle? Take time to create an Excel spreadsheet like the one provided that shows metrics for your church.

_____

_____

_____

_____

_____

_____

_____

_____

_____

_____

_____

_____

QUESTION 5— TEAM ALIGNMENT: *DO WE HAVE THE RIGHT PEOPLE IN THE RIGHT SEATS, MOVING THE RIGHT DIRECTION?*

If you don't fight for a healthy environment, then you will not be able to retain healthy leaders.

READING TIME

As you read Chapter 9: "Question 5—Team Alignment: Do We Have the Right People in the Right Seats, Moving the Right Direction?" in *When Your Church Feels Stuck*, review, reflect on, and respond to the text by answering the following questions.

REFLECT AND TAKE ACTION:

In your own words, how would you define team alignment?

_____

_____

_____

_____

_____

_____

_____

Is your team currently aligned? What happens when a team is misaligned?

_____

_____

_____

_____

_____

_____

_____

Have you ever avoided conflict and left someone ineffective in their position? If so, describe the situation.

_____

_____

_____

_____

_____

_____

_____

What happens to the team when a poor leader remains in his or her position?

_____

_____

_____

_____

_____

_____

_____

What qualities do you look for in new team members? Do you look for all ten of the qualities listed in this chapter?

_____

_____

_____

_____

_____

_____

What do you do to grow? Why is this so important for leaders to do?

_____

_____

_____

_____

_____

_____

Do you have the right people in the right seats? Is there anyone who shouldn't be where they are?

_____

_____

_____

_____

_____

_____

Is your team all moving in the same direction, or are they headed toward different goals?

_____

_____

_____

_____

_____

_____

QUESTION 6— CULTURE: *HOW DO WE CHANGE THE CULTURE OF OUR CHURCH?*

You can change the culture of your church, and if you do, you will win!

READING TIME

As you read Chapter 10: "Question 6—
Culture: How Do We Change the Culture of
Our Church?" in *When Your Church Feels
Stuck*, review, reflect on, and respond to the
text by answering the following questions.

REFLECT AND TAKE ACTION:

What is culture? Why is it important?

_____

_____

_____

_____

_____

_____

_____

What is your church's culture?

_____

_____

_____

_____

_____

_____

_____

_____

If you could change your church's culture in any way, how would you change it? What would you emphasize?

_____

_____

_____

_____

_____

_____

_____

_____

What part of your church is affected by culture? Are there any aspects of your church that are totally unaffected?

_____

_____

_____

_____

_____

_____

_____

_____

What have you done in recent months with your church's culture in mind?

_____

_____

_____

_____

_____

_____

_____

_____

How can you go about shaping and reshaping your church's culture? What are some practical ways your team can accomplish this?

_____

_____

_____

_____

_____

_____

_____

_____

What does it mean to "drive the culture"? How can you accomplish this in your church?

_____

_____

_____

_____

_____

_____

_____

_____

QUESTION 7— SERVICES:

HOW DO WE MATCH WHAT WE SAY IS IMPORTANT AND WHAT WE REALLY DO?

It's not about putting on a show. . . . It's about presenting the message of Jesus in a way that people far from God can connect and relate to.

READING TIME

As you read Chapter 11: "Question 7—Services: How Do We Match What We Say Is Important and What We Really Do?" in *When Your Church Feels Stuck*, review, reflect on, and respond to the text by answering the following questions.

REFLECT AND TAKE ACTION:

What is the average time your team takes to prepare and plan a service? Do you feel this is adequate?

_____

_____

_____

_____

_____

_____

_____

Is there room for a creative element in your services? Why or why not?

_____

_____

_____

_____

_____

_____

_____

_____

Have you ever used creative communication, creative elements, or planned a creative series? How do you think these could benefit your services?

_____

_____

_____

_____

_____

_____

_____

_____

_____

_____

What practical changes can you make to improve your services based on this chapter?

_____

_____

_____

_____

_____

_____

_____

_____

_____

_____

_____

_____

What will be your and your team's biggest takeaways from this book? What will be the first steps you take to get your church unstuck?

_____

_____

_____

_____

_____

_____

_____

_____

_____

_____

_____